WATUSI
TITANIC

WATUSI TITANIC

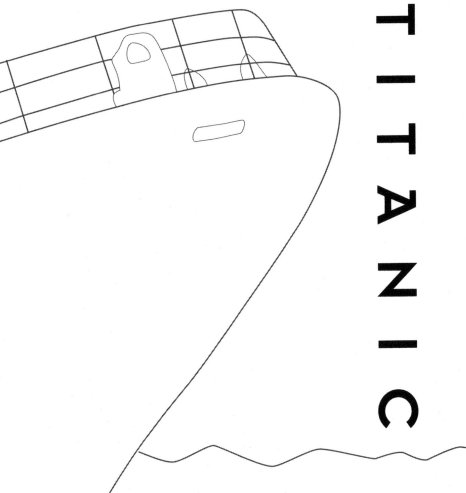

CONNIE DEANOVICH

TIMKEN PUBLISHERS

The author wishes to thank the editors of the following publications, in which these poems first appeared. "My Favorite Monk Is," *Parnassus* 19:2; "Plaid Into Conquest" and "Requirements for Suggesting Fats Waller," *Situation* 8; "Requirements for a Saint," *New American Writing* 13; "Circus Sestina," *B City* 8; "What's the Best Way to Live Here," "Virtue is not Photogenic," and "Athletic Competition" (previously "I've Just Returned from an Athletic Competition"), *New American Writing* 10; "Pure Valentine" and "Ballerina Criminology," *New American Writing* 1; "80 Degrees Out," "At the Car Mirror/Fuck 'Em County," and "Xylophone Luncheonette," *New American Writing* 2 ("Pure Valentine" and "Xylophone Luncheonette" anthologized in *Under 35: The New Generation of American Poets*, ed. Nicholas Christopher); "Dating Patton," "Road Block: Santa Fe New Mexico," and "The Narrator" (previously "Connie Deanovich"), *Colorado North Review* 33:1 & 2 ("The Narrator" and "Road Block: Santa Fe New Mexico" anthologized in *Walk on the Wild Side: Urban American Poetry Since 1975*, ed. Nicholas Christopher); "Nicola Tesla," *Exquisite Corpse* 44; "Pal Construction" (previously "Amvets has a White Tag Sale"), *Oink 17*; "Addition to Hitchcock," *New American Writing* 11; "Warning to Pirates," *No Roses Review* 1:1; "History as Bourgeois Construct" and "Watusi Titanic," *Sulfur* 31; "The Window" (previously "Thinks the Peeping Toms"), *Brooklyn Review* 7; "Dawn," *New American Writing* 4; "Spring Sestina" and "Old Shawneetown Illinois 1810-1960," *The Illinois Architectural and Historical Review*; "Shipwreck is Antique Frenzy," *The World* 48.

"Dating Patton," "Dawn," "Pal Construction" (previously "Amvets Has a White Tag Sale"), "Xylophone Luncheonette," "Ballerina Criminology," and "Arbus's 'A Young Man in Curlers at Home on West 20th Street, NYC, 1966'" also appeared in *Ballerina Criminology*, a chapbook published by The Pink Dog Press, Toronto, 1990.

The author also wishes to express thanks to the GE Foundation for a General Electric Foundation Award for Younger Writers and to my nominating editors Paul Hoover and Maxine Chernoff of *New American Writing* for their help throughout my career. For her help with this book, thanks is given to Caroline Knox. The emotional support of my correspondents and the financial assistance of The Fund for Poetry is also gratefully acknowledged.

Timken Publishers, Inc.
225 Lafayette Street,
New York, NY 10012

LIBRARY OF CONGRESS CATALOGUING-IN-PUBLICATION DATA
Deanovich, Connie, 1960–
    Watusi titanic / Connie Deanovich
        p.   cm.
    ISBN 0–943221–24–2 (pbk.)
    PS3554.E1744W38   1996
    811'.54—dc20

Poems set in Sabon, titles in Neuland Inline and Insignia
Cover and text designed and produced by David Bullen
Printed in the United States of America

for David

Contents

VIRTUE IS NOT PHOTOGENIC

THE CLOTHES OF THE SICK AND THE DEAD

REQUIREMENTS
FOR A SAINT

My Favorite Monk Is

raking leaves
brown as his robe
and he's the kind

who speaks (most
eloquently about
the vow of silence)

Language he says
is the skeleton
of the spirit

It's nice
to think of a skeleton
the Halloween kind

with a patch over one eye
as the bony place
where words

can shimmy
Inside
he bakes a chicken

in honey
and his house
is like other houses

on a regular block
Surrounding it
like a halo is

a garden
never tortured
by lawn decoration

At times
while working
in his yard

a drawbridge goes up
unexpectedly
and he catches

faint whiffs
of the stinky
flowers of hell

Requirements for a Saint

think of a saint
and you think
of the incredibly dull clothing of a saint

perhaps extreme temperatures
or the difficult *terrain* they travel
(everything about a saint draws attention to itself)

think of a saint
and your thought is not
of a train thrusting through lightning

but of wind that smells of wood
or a wet disease
(saint world is the world of the empty hand)

breath is sometimes banged out of copper
and so is a saint
often with bell attachments

I'll make you a saint
from an unblemished code book
that must be read

in a German restaurant
where beer is served in glasses
wrapped in brown leather

when the cuckoo strikes twelve
this will be the moment
of ascension

Requirements for the Visionary Cyclist

that the man wearing a monocle
is not a biker is axiomatic

complete your picture of him
in the nineteenth century

give him a bugle if happy
the vocabulary of balance if not

a woodchuck on his shoulder
is less disfiguring than resignation and

"double espresso *tames* me"
is a suitable quote

when it storms
let him change color like storefronts and

when this subsides
walk him into the distance

give him palm trees to look at
and a bike made from their wood

have him by bicycle
encircle the Taj Mahal

his response to it changing
with each revolution

Bach Beach

a couple promenades each night
and burns their sleep
in a bonfire fit for a king

the next day charred ruins remain
the hair and bones of half-burned dreams
sizzle in the tide water then float away to museums

the man has come to Bach Beach
to rid himself of all things ephemeral
and to set his confessions into stone

as he chisels
an opera dangles on a chain around his muscular neck
the woman has come to free herself from the need to sleep

which always makes her mutter embarrassing admissions
tonight, like a recovering ornithologist
she will burn her dreams of flying

then plot a chart of them
which will later be found in a cave
and taken to the archives of a great European university

Requirements for Suggesting Fats Waller

a stack of summer suits makes a better emblem than a piano
the sound of which lures a group of ambassadors to a tall fence

after opening the biggest brass door in Chicago
88 Girl Scouts celebrate overcoming obstacles
by wiping their brows in order of height

after combing her hair out to the ground
my grandmother sat very still
as if preparing to do The Carolina Shout or The Alligator Crawl
both of which end in frenzy but start in silence

put a few coins in
and a sweaty polka dotted neckerchief comes out

Requirements for the Large-Scale

If a dollop of army is spread
on the map of a ball
imagine the trajectory!
Even as concept
balls advance through air
precise as chant
stoked by the voices of monks.
Beauty though round

can also be narrowed for the sake of intent.
A huge rope dangling above a cargo ship
made of cardboard
shows the beauty of transiency
and the most mysterious cathedral
folds out of a letter, better still
if it comes smudged with fingerprints
suggesting adventures that remain incomplete.

Requirements for Satisfaction

pleasure slopes
notably
the devotion to it

then the black thickness
of ancient buildings
sees us through

stand forever next to me
not virtuously
just matter-of-factly

in trench coats
suddenly face to face
with some harsh reality

calm me down
give your recital of the reassuring formulaic
mechanism of the fugue

or else train my eye
with a little but successful meal
that begins and ends without an outline

the goal is
you become my border
when all other borders disappear

that's me waving now from the
disappearing doorway of a carnival fun house
where I've holed up like a villain

the goal is for you
to capture me
bring me handcuffed and squinting into the sunshine

the goal is for you
to play
my game

talk tensely
like a radio thespian
intrigue me this way

tell me the Shanghai Cobra
has stolen my jewels
that miniature bottles of memory

were left as a calling card
that tomorrow concentration becomes
dazzlingly complete

that I'll sit soft and still
like a rouged fortune teller
completely deluded by herself

completely believing in herself
in signs that come clutched
in a monkey's paw

or supported by the butchered
but once suppliant maiden
of a bad dream

you say I dream out loud
a nocturnal gift of gab
that's mostly screaming

the goal is for you
to keep the secrets that shoot
out of my head and

darken my sleep
with the crowning shadow
of an enormous palm

sleep must be awkward
for you too
but I count on you being old-fashioned

on you keeping sleep symmetrical
the way you lie there submerged
in the firm foundation of pleasure

and I want this near me
to run my hand through pleasure
and precision

to run my eye
over your presence
and your shadow

immemorial baseball games
when we're eating for nine
detesting other pleasures

are wrapped inside the cape too
black velvet lined with pink silk
that's best worn when it's raining in angles

Circus Sestina

A medieval triptych can't activate the senses
like a three-ring circus can: greasy acrobats
pitched out of cannons, tutu'd dogs
tiptoeing in wheelbarrows. A conversation
between circus freaks is often about eating.
No one talks in shadows about tomorrow.

In the "World of Tomorrow"
tent, recorded talk about the rising census
dominates. We'll be eating
very little, bodies slim as acrobats,
"how to survive" everyone's conversation.
It will be illegal to own a dog.

But I *am* thinking of getting a dog
if not today, then tomorrow.
A dog is more fun than conversazione
and certainly does more for the senses—
those fluffy, loyal, Frisbee acrobats
whose interests lie mostly in eating.

Cardamom for the sensorium is what I call eating.
The scent of a good Indian meal can dog
you for days. If a crow bats
glossy wings above the Standard India Restaurant tomorrow,
love interests will start to make sense
and romance will honeycoat conversation.

A circus fortune teller guarantees this astounding conversation
and creates in you a great desire to be eating
Indian food. With peanuts in hand, this makes little sense,
but as you move on, you are driven to obey like a dog

and will visit Standard India tomorrow
where aromatic mustard seeds splatter, the acrobats

of spice. Reeking of doom, a blindfolded acrobat
closes her trailer door, a conversation
piece by itself: black as her idea of tomorrow,
windows misted by smoke, rust eating
away at the metal, a mad dog
chained to a chain. Overloaded senses

made her a prisoner of her senses. Acrobats
descend then unwind. Dogs circle garbage. Conversation
and eating cease. Circus closed until tomorrow.

STATES
OF THE BODY

What's the Best Way to Live Here?

Resuscitate clemency?
Move like a loom across the social spectrum?
Imagine a lady
slightly mildewed
beside the white chickens,
should we treat her,
like a burning candle,
to a windless alcove
a place to look down upon
the sinking canoe?
Or should we bury her
like a hellhound
in unconsecrated ground
rub glass in her memory
like a smarmy optimist playing
The Illinois Lottery?

What charm works best here?
A stack of calligraphied chants
tall as a hypnotized woman?
A smoked chanteuse
upon a stumbling elephant?

Skies determine activity
and inactivity's best
a day spent receiving letters
in the breezeway of a retired
Hell's Angel with stories

With apricots and a book on
the Ice Age
whole mornings can wash down

the muddy Activity River like
a flood of Louisianas

What historical piano fits best here?
The one Jerry Lee Lewis broke his thumb on
or the miniature Bosendorfer
Horowitz carried on his key ring?

Should the music match
the prickling sensation of a sexual alcohol rub
or pang weakly like a Serbian
alcoholic in a death march?

What harbinger best describes tomorrow here?
The reddened windows keeping the color in kissing
or the green darkness that warns
of a measles epidemic?

We are bidding you for answers
we who have learned to eat peas with a knife
we who elevate hard labor as if it were
a hard body

And now our hard city
is softening like a lobotomized criminal
and we smile
as if we hear voices and a sharply tuned
violin that distracts us from
our great mistakes

Pure Valentine

In the orchestra it matters. Beards
become concerns as if it were a circus with dollars to be made
where everyone wakes up at sunrise,
gets cold with barn water, so their singing voices drop down
for a song sung importantly
to a low flower.

This is never done in a hamlet where
mothers come home on stretchers after a nightshift on the switchboard.
Awake, all voices sound big,
the diapason clear as in the best city's best auditorium
where all audiences are royal
or feel so feeling muted velvet on their cold necks.

Next to a closet kneels a boy
wanting to be inside, light a candle to undress Barbie dolls by,
and to read how Xygon, the Ibu prince, got his power, and
can he have some? His
brains creak now, take him to a cold tower,
acquit him of piano lessons,
nimble fingers better used on snaps
and strings, plastic pumps and tiny teacups.

Later, he is protected by geese on the soft edge of a windy lake.
It matters here that there be wind to cool his hot hair,
to teach him to use it for trumpet time, to slurp up air
like good dope smoke savored, then release something better,
bluer.

The truth is only practiced, not perfected to flaw
until you wear off-white and love a man named Devotion,
build a cool kitchen with free cats circumventing

like a seam on a purple yellow sari you watched spinning
as it stood on a bus.

In Rome how lost you'd be in antiquity with new people
reading newspapers upside down
and no genetics to weave a blonde for you to wink at.

It would have to be a boat
to justify your coming back here.

Athletic Competition

"There's a lot of glamour here tonight," Carnell said
And there was
The bar that on Tuesday held an urban softball team
on Saturday was the haunt of lesbians too glamorous
to throw the ball

Unless it was in slow motion
and loose hair could be seen
falling across a coral mouth
half open

But the *here*
was way after the real ball game
which was also glamorous
but in a different sense

There
men were glamorous
and beyond reach
reaching for the ball
in quick slow motion with
chest muscles
stretching up like
satellites

I return from these
scenes of glamour
in name only
speckled with wisps
of glamorous mud from the Wheel of Fortune
status symbol of the dirt road
that leads to paths of glory

Spring Sestina

anticipation crooked in a cage
no longer ice brave
hand a dried out jewel
lung in tin
winter rattling "still have you Illinois"
and there's no baseball

and there will be no baseball
no pin-striped slugger in a batting cage
no *real* White Sox in Chicago Illinois
no home of the brave
heart of tin
action a jewel

spring shipwrecked like *The Mississippi Jewel*
in the seasonal slammer playing rec-yard baseball
flipping tin
pacing a cage
embroidering B-R-A-V-E
the penitentiary Joliet Illinois

where is Spring Explodes Illinois?
take this whispering jewel
to Miss Verna Brave
hide it inside an experienced baseball
exchange it for a bronze key to this gray cage
go stealthily clothed dull as tin

when these skies of tin
over the frozen lump of Illinois
swing open like an operatic cage
and the soprano of fat spring touches her jewels

and hits a high C farther than a mid-high baseball
the deal's gone through with Miss Verna Brave

but now pain distresses the brave
who sit on frozen tin
and cocktail away the promise of baseball
or who are eating all the pizza in Illinois
and reading *The Big Creepy Book of Ugly People's Jewels*
frozen feet soaking in an epsom salt cage

massive cage for the no longer brave
divide into a jewel as bronze divides into copper and tin
and Illinois divides into winter and time for baseball

80 Degrees Out

I may become a bum today,
sit on the Nathan Hale statue
smoking pot, practicing

neck exercises like a healthy
nun. Oh blast of gym whistles,
hijack this bus to Ohio

so I can see a weather vane
twist like a court trial
lost in a barn. The

countryside, that's where
real weather lives, naming
its alphabetical hurricanes

Abigail and Bridget. Camille,
you vocalist from the Volga,
whose braids spiders climb, I sniff

glue and become you, a janissary
infant nearly leprous by lunchtime.
A Lenten meal of cabbage and beans

may clean you out by motherly mandate,
though one swallowed marble would
do the same. Spring is a

solar slut is not a nice thing
to coo to a kitten, but it's
great ceremony for christening

ships, something darker
to spill than champagne. It's
hot in my pillory, and I need it

more than a ship, need to nautical
on out of here by the light of
an opera and sleep by the great wet lake.

Dating Patton

When I'm too busy
I pretend
I'm dating Patton

Battle-scarred
triumphant
exhausted
and pissed

we couple
a couple of
war horses
big on the scene
in our own minds

not minding
wind
snow
veracity

we say anything
to get it done
we feel anything
to get it done

and when we're
done with each
other

spent
like sparklers

we plant ourselves
in the ground
like neurotic Dobermans

leaving a mark
waiting to grow
again

into two
supreme
pains in the ass

Nicola Tesla

An unpredictable man
grew from a boy who
wanted to fly in a machine
he kept in his mind
and powered with June bugs

Pearl earrings made him vomit
germs infected his moustache
only 18 napkins at the side of his
plate would bring him to eat

To friends, he was as predictable as the mathematics
that sailed through his mind like feathers

Maybe that's why he loved pigeons
who always flock in numbers to the hand that feeds them

One bird really
set his spinnaker going

"I loved her," he wrote
"as a man loves a woman
and she loved me

"As long as I had her
there was purpose in my life"

Unlike Edison
whose mind was shore bound
he never electrocuted a dog
and he was unfit for romance

He was once almost
boiled alive in a vat of hot milk
but he died alone in a hotel room

The chartered
way for a misfit who changed the
course of the world
to leave it

The electrical genius born in a storm

Xylophone Luncheonette

We began to dance
and soon
what got you strong
is what I loved

We'll own this place
and paint a sign for I-90:
Free Coffee and Donut
To Honeymooners

We stand
in party corners
drinkin' white lightning

We want to own a luncheonette
crimp pickles
shake chips
melt cheese on white toast
ice parsley &
music a mood
frantic as barn love

You're my lucky penny
got me off the highway crew
shorn my wig

Took me uptown
watched my shimmy said

Now

That's all right

States of the Body

COMMERCE

When
I
worked
at
Marsh
all
Fields
as a
floater
in the
cosmet
ics
depart
ment
the
one
counte
r I
hated
was
the
one
that
sold
the
stuff
severel
y
birthm
arked

people
bought
to
cover
up
their
birthm
arks or
the
damag
e to
their
skin a
disastr
ous
fire
caused

the
reason
I hated
this
counte
r was
becaus
e the
cosmet
ics
stoppe
d
being
fun
and

even
though
as a
young
white
chick I
was
not
real
qualifi
ed to
work
the
Fashio
n Fair
counte
r either
I much
preferr
ed
being
unqual
ified
there
where
the
black
women
pitied
me
and
selecte
d their
own

shades
of
brown
withou
t my
clumsy
sugges
tions
than to
work
at the
birthm
ark
counte
r
where
even
men
came
to buy
the
produc
ts
essenti
al to
their
lives

LOVE

Because he listened to the Sex Pistols
then switched to Landowska playing Bach's
Inventions on harpsichord, wore a strange, unbusinessy
black suit all the time and a different scarf every time, never hit me
or called me a name, ate like a pig with the taste buds of a refined
American tasting machine or a Frenchgirl born to a gifted cook
of a father, danced in BIG leather boots quite light-footedly, could
explain sunshine, was first spotted wearing chains and drinking
Coke, never drove a car but borrowed one to see me, wrote music
using counterpoint and mathematics, and . . . (say it with
me now) had a great sense of humor:

I thought he couldn't be real.

That the *pink* quarter-sized triangular birthmark on his right
hand meant he was a Martian or at least a future psycho who
would ruin my life. And because I've been married to him for
many years I have to now sometimes look at his Martian Mark, as
we have been calling it ever since my (red-faced) confession early
on, in order to remember that he is

mysterious and fine.

POLITICS

My father has a scar on his forehead from when he had a tumor removed from his brain. I took possession of this scar on my ninth birthday. The scar is round, the size of a tester pancake. It is an indentation on his skull about 1/8th of an inch deep. Running from the round indentation is a gash, the knife wound. Together they look like the number nine collapsing. I noticed this brain tumor scar on my ninth birthday and thanked my father for carving the number nine onto his head in honor of me. Even though he still laughs at my gratitude, deep inside I continue to believe it is true. Gorbachev reminds me of my father, a Serb who was also a citizen of an eastern European bloc country. When I looked at Gorbachev's face I admired his birthmark because it reminded me of my father's scar. I am certain that he can tell a family story about his disfigurement. I would listen to it even though I never listened to his speeches.

Fuck 'Em County

Go with the basket
find a rock to adore
to be your woman
your heavy clarity
heavy as a stack of 78s
and the rock I throw through them
Rock around the fucking clock
Oh come on
Like
give me orange pantyhose man
I'll rock
I'll show you who's queen of the county
At Bird's Drive-In
At the corner spot
At the car mirror
see my lips, pooch
shine your headlights on 'em
they're not even red
When you're through peeking
just go with the basket
find a rock to adore
to be your woman

Pal Construction

When I think of it,
the south side practically bites my ear,
and earrings,
and I can't help seeing a store
selling a bust of a dunce at an enormous price.
It is slow like a ship,
and catches me in its big signs,
PAL CONSTRUCTION,
its small grandmas,
and makes me remember that I am
south side,
a girl who's mouth got in the way at suppertime.
It's the Land of the Big Hot Dog,
the Golden Tiara Bingo Hall,
with stoves for sale on the sidewalk,
cheap, but pink.
How wonderful a delicate factory
can look to me,
though it may be loud as morning,
and next to a garden.
You can tell by its peep shows
that the south side is dated,
SEE A LADY IN A CAGE.
But I like it, and can't help pointing.
Thundering ballrooms,
elegance is a banana curl on a Spanish head,
a hopeful photograph of baby sleeping,
cute, but pink.
I am happy with my hand again on the old beam;
see the tank in the park?

VIRTUE
IS NOT
PHOTOGENIC

Arbus's "A Young Man in Curlers at Home on West 20th Street, NYC, 1966"

A young man
at home
in curlers

Could be any street
any city
but not
any sitter
not

every 40 year old
long-faced
like El Greco
urbanite
eye-

brows plucked
like parentheses
silver
fingernailed
like a Hunt brother
and

smoking
while he seems
to say

"Look!
I live
here

I'm
at
home

I
don't care
if you take my picture

What
do you
want
it for?

Sure!
why not?

What's curlers?

Want coffee?"

But a museum visitor
actually
says

"*That*
is scary"
and

turns away
combing
her hair
that's

feathered
and pink
less generous

but why not
she's young

and away from the home
she'll sit
still in someday
older and

unabashed

Addition to Hitchcock

on an evening just like this many years ago
Susan moved into a new apartment

it was raining
and it was going to rain

she had three big windows that overlooked an avenue
across the street was a laundromat and a pizza parlor

she opened the windows and sat on an ugly couch
the previous tenant left there

it was orange and had suspicious stains on it
it was positioned so that the sitter could look out the windows

rain air blew in on her as she sat wondering
she got up and wheeled her television over

she positioned it symmetrically
right in front of the middle window

exactly buttressed by the other two
the sky darkened

the apartment darkened
Susan popped in *The Birds*

she watched it and the storm at the same time
even with this addition

she was unable to fathom whether the love birds
had anything to do with the terrible tragedy or not

she decided that next time she would wheel her TV
down to the cellar and watch *The Birds* from there

and if that didn't work she'd buy a Watchman and
watch on a bus that lumbered through a dangerous neighborhood

tomorrow though she would set the TV in the middle of a table
and have two youths from the community center

play ping-pong on it while she watched the
little white ping-pong arc sweetly over

Suzanne Pleshette's head in the schoolyard scene
that's dipped first in so much tenderness then in so much blood

Ballerina Criminology

To be cold as a ballerina in a trap,
finally worn out by fluttering,
made me rethink the possibilities,
a murder or just one staged for
the sake of the jewels.

Ten minutes before dinner with the sexy Communist
someone turned me over in the ditch,
and now your guest list is wanted.

Who, especially, prayed by the pines?

Out she danced from the gypsy wagon,
snapping a fan and a smile to
generalize honesty. Something taped
to her thigh, in honor of the German,
brought the American quickly round
to nod for the dream maidens to disappear her
into the drape he saved for his snake.

Warning to Pirates

Pirates, if you dare to think
of the vastness
of the precious horizonless sea
on which you sail
and think of things like this:
hats black as slate
the red and green of your
perfect black eye
yellow nets enclosing blue acres
of tuna
which fit neatly into silver cans
and are sold as small parcels
on the huge continent of North America
on a dull grocers shelf
and are bought by a stripper keeping thin
who does "the peel" for a living

If you dare to think this
you will not see
the vastness
the precious horizonless sea
so, pirates, leave your imagination out of it
for the pirate who dares to think
in terms of color
finds himself growing shore legs
finds himself no longer a pirate
finds he is enclosed by gray sellers
not rosy compilers of tuna
and by white lights from towns
where all vision is reworked
to suit the requirements of landlubbers:
all vision is less fancy

than the doormat under life at sea that is corroded
with jewel-green algal formations
all vision rises up
like white swan's down in a breeze
that swept inland from the sea
and is now, pirates, shorebound forever
all vision defined by inches not acres
all vision parcelled out
and nothing large enough to sink pirates in
nothing more visually dramatic
than the colorful pirates themselves
no bread as ocean wave image to soak up pirate gravy
no sea to diminish a pirate
nothing to make them anything less than the biggest
image on the scene:
the pirate expanding his telescope at the bank
the pirate scratching scale off his patch over the sink
the one-legged pirate at the symphony recalling
monochromatic war to his multicolored parrot

The pirate who longs for the sea itself
and not ideas of the sea
is the pirate who heeds this warning
and sets out to find a ship
the *Lady Misery*
the *Young World*
the *Moral Witness*
the *Devil's Mansion*
so long as there's rope and water
sky and sea
so long as there's everything required

History as Bourgeois Construct

when they lived on
    El Burrito Magnifico
    and in leopard skins
    with bulky buttons

when across the living room
    the light of the el
    swept swift
    as white glove over
    dusty mantle

when the wine bar was
    Whiskey Heaven

when shirt sleeves
    carried the pollen
    of quick sex and got
    the whole group groping

when oranges were sliced
    as the only hors d'oeuvre

when dancing and walking equalled
    Life Itself and
    reading was done by pink lamp light
    emanating from a black ballerina lamp
    such an out-of-fashion pursuit
    so much the fan
    of silent movies and Grant Wood

poor History is now a "bourgeois construct"
    running green water into

the red barn
elemental   elemental

when things broke down
    into elements as ephemeral as black lace at noon

when *Psycho* with its black bra and taxidermy vision
    was the mansion for imagination's dirt
    imagination must have dirt
    black billy clubs walled and lit by an enthusiastic masochist
    prayer must be a part for some

when every home entered had a pastel plastic shrine to Jesus

when the man who roams Clark Street
    roams it again look
    how he looks like he's 80
    except for a jet-black pompadour

except that a friend has a compulsion to kiss locks
    he's great at a baseball game
    remembering is so important

how the opening of a pelican's eye
    is reminiscent of the eye
    of a creepy little drinking kid

when to the party they brought their kid
    and let it eat cat food

when the window opened
    onto the brick wall
    we called the house Brick View

large flames mean large history
    so clouds in the shape of luggage
    transport the smoke of
    where there's smoke there's
    malfunction
    dry seas
    Marlon Brando tap dancing

anything military ruins anything visionary
    anything organized by history
    gets the curled lip

when events are dunked
    into the neutral milk of history
    how hard can it be to say
    this came before that
    without purposefully smearing the tracks

Road Block: Santa Fe, New Mexico

I had good manners
and waited until we passed
before taking pictures from Kathy's car

The policemen
in Nazi-black rubber gloves
and boots, double-barrelled shotguns
poised behind semis

so hot
not a tree in sight
no water, little sound
adobe-penitentiary glazing in heat
just before the mesa went red

This is too western
way too meaty
like a pig baked underground

I'm selling my square of the blanket
Jimenez was found in
and the patch of Governor's grass
where the last one died crouching

This is too western
I'm selling my pictures—
a pushed-back policemen's hat radioing in
the red flashlight waving us on

The Window

She has a window in her chest
and we see what she desires—
someone *else* who'll rotate her tires.

The tires go round and round
like black tumbleweeds
on a green trampoline

and she just sits and waits for them
on a black plastic car-wash chair
reading a book called *Desire.*

We see a white woman's chest heaving on the cover.
She's in the arms of her
black pirate lover who,

on top of a green bed,
will soon rotate *her* tires.
The window shows us this

and then another thought
holograms the book one out.
It's "Let's Go Fly a Kite,"

and the woman is a nanny,
wow. She's so starched—so navy,
polished like a bank.

Her kite is colorfully extravagant though:
it's the AIDS quilt.
Goodbye, nanny.

A new picture now,
the tires again,
pulling into a tunnel of total blackness.

Oh, now there's light.
But we *could* read
her thoughts with Braille.

But to touch would get us green.
So we just stand in the dark
at the window.

Virtue is Not Photogenic

no nun ever turned a head
the way Humphrey Bogart did
even when sucking a string
of meat out from between his teeth
he's interesting looking
perhaps especially then
and although my mother would poo-poo
the idea, citing the innocence of her
generation, maybe all that sucking and
mumbling and throwing back whiskeys was
an early early prepunk fuck you to the
world and yours attitude and so my
mom and then all of us sort of swooned
at his photogenic unvirtuousness

in Chaucer School
everybody says the Nun's Priest's Tale
is the best and why? because it's bad
and in our minds before photography even
the picture looked better if it
depicted something bad

we love the bad because in films
and stories it's so pretty, not
Robert Blake in *In Cold Blood* bad
but Humphrey Bogart bad
as the bad knight Philip Marlowe

From *The Big Sleep* on,
my god how I love the bad boys who
were actually better than the real
bad boys. The unvirtuous photogenic

from Humphrey Bogart to Mick Jagger.
And although again she'd dismiss me for loving
Humphrey even with his unhip square name and
Mick Jagger at the same time, my mom
never saw *Gimme Shelter* when Mick shouted "Who's
fighting and what for? Come on! Come on!
We don't want to fight!"

There's not much difference
imaginatively between his speech and
Humphrey's "stick 'em up, wise guys"
because for all the toughness there
both reassure us that the badness we
carry inside us is good to have.
Without pretty badness, men seem invisible
and pale, and god how I hate wimps
and would if I could
blow them down like a sea goddess
but only when my mother's not looking

Weegee's "Arrested for
Bribing Basketball Players, 1942"

In the
iron
elevator
three men wipe
their faces
away
become
fedora
hats
and
Palm Springs
tie
pinky
ring
and alcoholic teeth
busting
a
bottom
lip
they ride
to the basement
symbolically

THE CLOTHES
OF THE SICK
AND THE DEAD

Watusi Titanic

an Atlantic Ocean White
                    dress
        hangs in the window
                        catching a breeze

    the way the Atlantic Ocean Goers

in formal dress

    hang beautifully underwater

                catching seaweed

they tried to catch their breaths

    like a Watusi on the basketball court

        but they

    unlike him
                didn't

            in
                it wouldn't
    out
        was another matter

there's nothing the matter with thinking

            of the

    beauty of Watusi genetics and its implication

on the NBA

or with thinking about the

beauty of *Titanic* dead and how this implies

a certain onlyness

in the way "round like a chicken"

implies that chickens are only thought of as dead

and Watusi is thought of only

in the same breath as *jungle* never *stadium*

and *Titanic* means sunk

Watusi tall

once not sunk but tall

the young *Titanic* shot hoops through frozen white waves

for once not tall but

sunk under warm blue waves

a young Watusi man swims

casting a watery shadow only

a great ghost ship could eclipse

Blue Cuisine

blue cuisine
is served
in the municipal swimming pool

thin glass noodles
in thick blue sauce
draw
into the water treader's
mouths
followed by lush swallows
of grape juice
sloshing in glass goblets
big as Biblical beehives

the natatorium
is quietly abuzz
with a hundred swimmers
sucking down
blue cuisine

the lights
are turned off
to conserve the
vulnerable sensation
of blue eating
while
up to their necks
in echoing water

each swimmer
treads alone
like a great big orphan

tap dancing for pennies
on the $4,000 table
of the neighborhood industrialist

although he eats
great portions of brown food
to this monkey entertainment
his mood remains blue
and he sits
beside the solidity
of the grandfather clock
that sets the strokes
of his evening

Plaid into Conquest

Bone Figurine of White Castle Lady
(with black eye and
five years service button)
floats in a bottle of coconut cologne
and serves the matador well

he keeps it in his brocade pocket
where he used to keep the bone chip
of an actual saint

he is a success
and lives a thrilling life
in a town called Topless
in a neighborhood called Torched to the Ground

in the off season
he makes it his job
to study the phenomenon of the plaid bikini
with special attention paid to the buckle below the navel

the matador imagines
that even an American woman
in a plaid bikini
who was basted with water
from the River Nile
would match the vivaciousness
of his cape
and would similarly use on him
ancient movements of seduction

The Clothes of the Sick and the Dead

from the thrift store
we wear the clothes
of the sick and the dead

the lemon yellow pantsuit
worn previously through
many years of sexual indecision

the white mesh golf hat that
"protected" its former wearer from skin cancer
while making a happy-go-lucky statement

belts and shoes and purses
brown, emblazoned, and cracking
leather as forest-beaten as Robin Hood

who cares if those Levis
were seen last flying off a motorcycle
or if the bow tie was, apparently, cut off with a steak knife

for ninety cents a thick sweater can cover a bad stomach
twenty-five cent sunglasses can create an underground aura
and everything else in the store, apparently, matches

on the sad, straw-haired mannikin from the sixties
the highly-ranked Salvation Army clerk creates visions
and, the ensembles *can* be said to match

so select dark slacks
and top them with a pajama top
be clothed

and as a consequence
of choice
embody their memories

The Walk of Shame

begins at 7
in a flurry of feathers
when the big beautiful redhead

leaves the apartment
dressed in mint green leather
thin as leaves

the bright sun is too bright
happy joggers in ski caps pass too happy
accompanied by noisy dogs who are smiling

in a cloth bag from the library
she carries her sleep
its arms and feet are taped together

and its head is in a black hood
still, her sleep is comfortable
there in the book bag

where it is dreaming
of a silent canoe ride by moonlight
and the lack of a name

Blazon in Six

thirty-nine monologues
by thirty-nine witty people of various ages
but let me hear *you* like rain on the lawn
your voice that when threatened
transforms into a physical presence

Concerto in E Minor
Op. 11 for piano and orchestra by Chopin
and behind your ear
skin soft as a slice of lust

1840–1880
and your eye blue as gas flame
examines the Gothic Revivals
eyebrows like windows extended into gables

one hundred dollars is sweet mercy
so is your hand
stretched across the slippery rocks
like a formalist aesthetic
and so redefining them

twelve Indian, ninety-six Mexican,
one Afghanistani, fourteen Thai,
forty-six sushi, one Serbian restaurant
to choose from
or else stand barefoot making your spectacular salad
the legs so just in their proportions

pages 19–37
of *Mushrooms: a Golden Rule*
read by you in the decaying garden
your shadow warped by celestial alignment

Dawn

Naked is the song provoked by law

and the no "Oh Solo Mio" law is one of them.

So, in lush green fields telepathy instead

and for background only buzzing bees

across a hot dog bun. Lush green

dish water leads to a hand silvered

in the dream-blue light of Chester's Tattoo Parlor,

and, as parlor maid, Chester's fat daughter,

Dawn, smelling of bacon, gifted telepathically.

When she looks at you through her black bangs,

she doesn't need to sing it. You hear it:

"Ohhhhh solo mio," and turn away, provoked by the

law, silvering her palm with a Kennedy. Lush

and green, her cheeks then glow in the little parlor.

Old Shawneetown Illinois 1810–1960

Because it once haughtily refused Chicago a loan because
it thought it too puny

Shawneetown died

that and
because the Ohio River coats it each spring with
big
sloppy
unwanted
kisses
like from a psychopath celebrating his tongue

The Greek Revival Shawneetown bank building will

never revive
will instead calcify

is already a mythical past you can walk on

five 32-foot Doric columns and 16 grand steps

which might all collapse
obliterating what little is left—

the industry of assumptions
fueled by a frightened heartbeat
that assures you'll stay alive
when every dead thing here
contradicts this before your eyes

Visit here and visit alone

the ruins of southern Illinois
are not celebrated

merely confined
like some national embarrassment
behind a mossy retaining wall that
for years now
is about to give way at any moment

Shipwreck is Antique Frenzy

which in others goes best with a green moon
or a mist spiralling through a crack in the door

for me is best with a shipwreck
then common *frenzy* becomes antique frenzy

and I can place it reverentially on a black pedestal
for better glimpses of its wounds

to see sleepy regulation seafarers become a red
stripe of livestock tossing on sharp ocean waves

in a shipwreck bodies equal objects
chips of goat twist like insomniacs

disposable Rothschilds silver then plunge
like untrained torch singers under a temporary moon

heads that solidly scream
tatter nonetheless

to see a letter begun in the night
float without a bottle

the happy words *fit in my bathing suit again*
dissolving in a swirl of black foam

The Narrator

I am a woman in a red blouse
blushing to have to admit my
glowing autumn moon

has left the large backyard I
live in in my mind
There's a truck there now
yellow and black like a can

of tobacco
Idling
its engines are ready to burn

to blaze across the country
like resurrection sunshine

My books are in this truck:
Alice in Wonderland
Go Ask Alice
The Autobiography of Alice B. Toklas
Alice Ordered Me to be Made
and the rest

I'm shipping them to a tiny library
in Truth or Consequences, New Mexico
so that I can begin the life that
starts with apple picking and
ends with zigzagging down the street

Then I'll be a woman in a red blouse
blushing to have to admit my adventures
have landed me in a novel that makes

my friend a million dollars in
R-rated movie rights

The glowing autumn movie screen
at the drive-in will entertain the
truckers who idle away two hours

chewing tobacco and watching my life
on the giant fireproof screen
blazing momentarily like
a temperamental crystal in the
temperamental sunshine